THIS BOOK

Belongs to..

....

....

ANTI-RACISM BEGINNING WITH ME!

Note for parents when the children under 5 years:

At this age, children may begin to notice and point out differences in people they see around them. As a parent, you have the opportunity to gently lay the foundation of their worldview. Use language that's age-appropriate and easy for them to understand.

1. Recognize and celebrate differences – If your child asks about someone's skin colour, you can use it as an opportunity to acknowledge that people do indeed look different, but to point out things we have in common. You could say, "We are all human, but we are all unique, isn't that amazing"!

2. Be open – Make it clear that you're always open to your children'questions and encourage them to come to you with them. If your children point out people who look different – as young children can often do from curiosity – avoid shushing them or they will start to believe that it's a taboo topic.

3. Use fairness – Children, especially those around 5, tend to understand the concept of fairness quite well. Talk about racism as unfair and that's why we need to work together to make it better.

RS...

The back page of each coloring page is blank to prevent ink bleed into the next illustration.

"DARKNESS CANNOT DRIVE OUT DARKNESS,
ONLY LIGHT CAN DO THAT.
HATE CANNOT DRIVE OUT HATE,
ONLY LOVE CAN DO THAT"

"DARKNESS CANNOT DRIVE OUT DARKNESS,
ONLY LIGHT CAN DO THAT.
HATE CANNOT DRIVE OUT HATE,
ONLY LOVE CAN DO THAT"

"DARKNESS CANNOT DRIVE OUT DARKNESS,
ONLY LIGHT CAN DO THAT.
HATE CANNOT DRIVE OUT HATE,
ONLY LOVE CAN DO THAT"

"DARKNESS CANNOT DRIVE OUT DARKNESS,
ONLY LIGHT CAN DO THAT.
HATE CANNOT DRIVE OUT HATE,
ONLY LOVE CAN DO THAT"

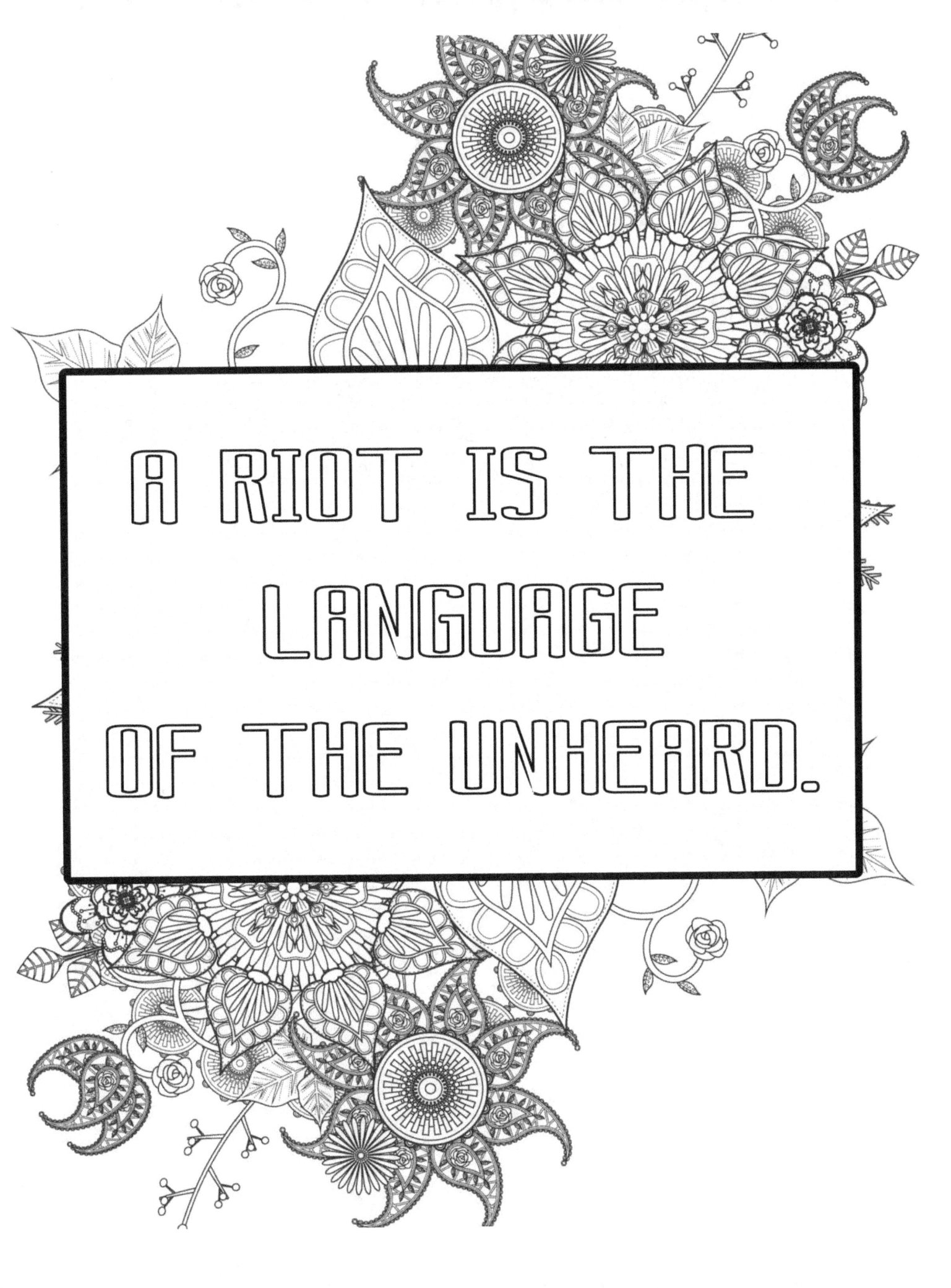

"DARKNESS CANNOT DRIVE OUT DARKNESS,
ONLY LIGHT CAN DO THAT.
HATE CANNOT DRIVE OUT HATE,
ONLY LOVE CAN DO THAT"

"DARKNESS CANNOT DRIVE OUT DARKNESS,
ONLY LIGHT CAN DO THAT.
HATE CANNOT DRIVE OUT HATE,
ONLY LOVE CAN DO THAT"

"DARKNESS CANNOT DRIVE OUT DARKNESS,
ONLY LIGHT CAN DO THAT.
HATE CANNOT DRIVE OUT HATE,
ONLY LOVE CAN DO THAT"

IF YOU WANT TO MAKE PEACE, YOU DON'T TALK TO YOUR FRIENDS. YOU TALK TO YOUR ENEMIES.

"DARKNESS CANNOT DRIVE OUT DARKNESS,
ONLY LIGHT CAN DO THAT.
HATE CANNOT DRIVE OUT HATE,
ONLY LOVE CAN DO THAT"

"DARKNESS CANNOT DRIVE OUT DARKNESS,
ONLY LIGHT CAN DO THAT.
HATE CANNOT DRIVE OUT HATE,
ONLY LOVE CAN DO THAT"

"DARKNESS CANNOT DRIVE OUT DARKNESS,
ONLY LIGHT CAN DO THAT.
HATE CANNOT DRIVE OUT HATE,
ONLY LOVE CAN DO THAT"

"DARKNESS CANNOT DRIVE OUT DARKNESS,
ONLY LIGHT CAN DO THAT.
HATE CANNOT DRIVE OUT HATE,
ONLY LOVE CAN DO THAT"

"DARKNESS CANNOT DRIVE OUT DARKNESS,
ONLY LIGHT CAN DO THAT.
HATE CANNOT DRIVE OUT HATE,
ONLY LOVE CAN DO THAT"

"DARKNESS CANNOT DRIVE OUT DARKNESS,
ONLY LIGHT CAN DO THAT.
HATE CANNOT DRIVE OUT HATE,
ONLY LOVE CAN DO THAT"

"DARKNESS CANNOT DRIVE OUT DARKNESS,
ONLY LIGHT CAN DO THAT.
HATE CANNOT DRIVE OUT HATE,
ONLY LOVE CAN DO THAT"

"DARKNESS CANNOT DRIVE OUT DARKNESS,
ONLY LIGHT CAN DO THAT.
HATE CANNOT DRIVE OUT HATE,
ONLY LOVE CAN DO THAT"

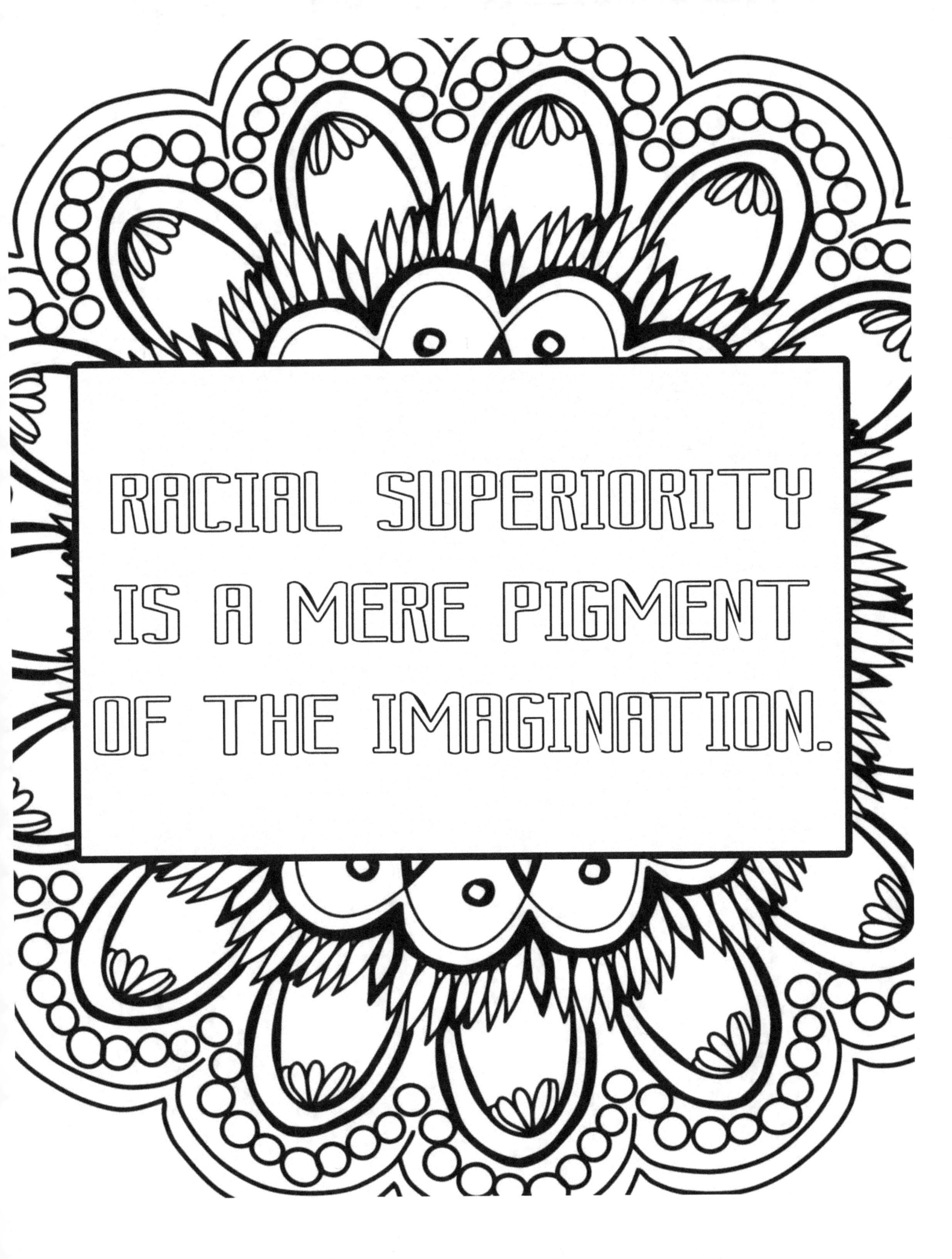

"DARKNESS CANNOT DRIVE OUT DARKNESS,
ONLY LIGHT CAN DO THAT.
HATE CANNOT DRIVE OUT HATE,
ONLY LOVE CAN DO THAT"

"DARKNESS CANNOT DRIVE OUT DARKNESS,
ONLY LIGHT CAN DO THAT.
HATE CANNOT DRIVE OUT HATE,
ONLY LOVE CAN DO THAT"

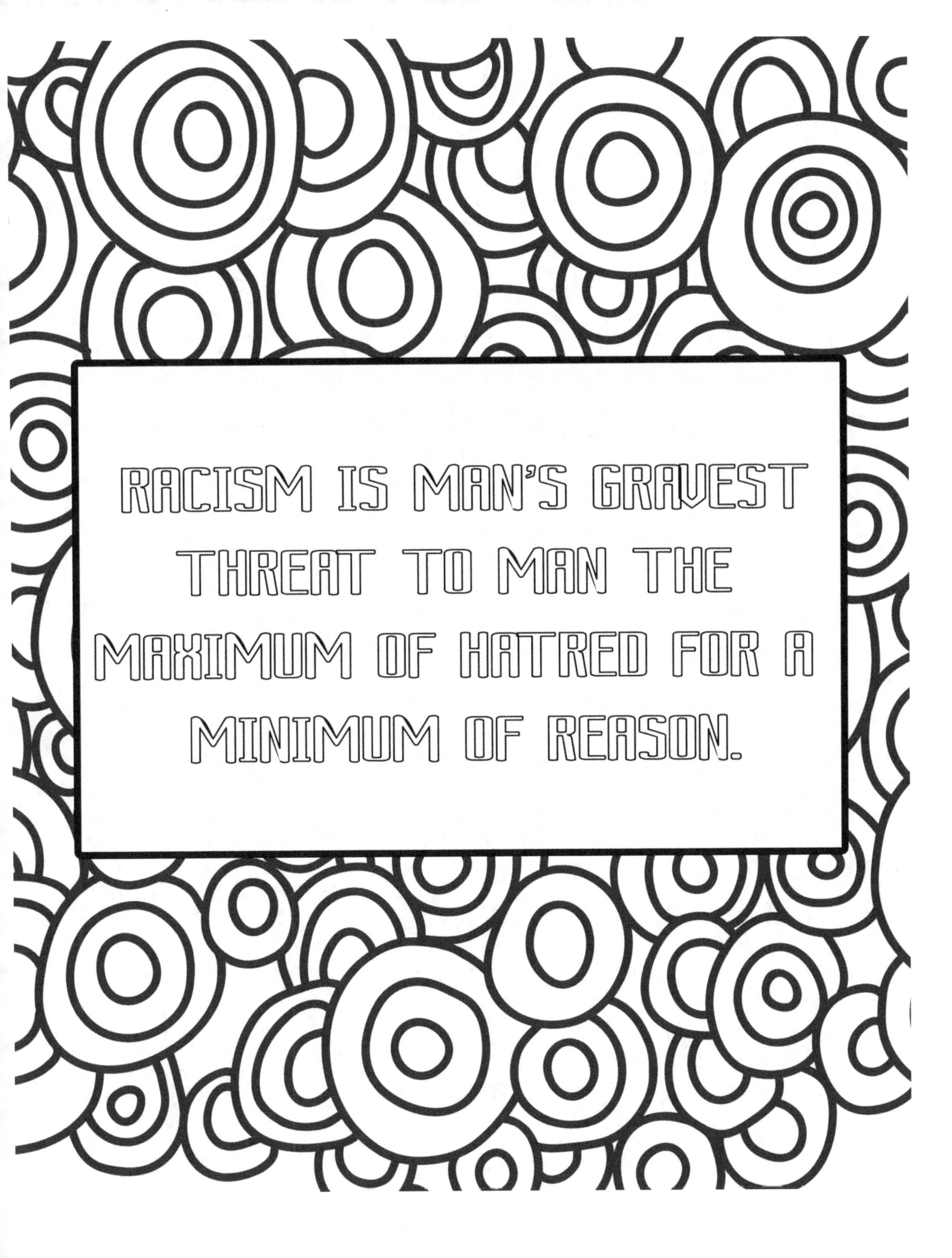

"DARKNESS CANNOT DRIVE OUT DARKNESS,
ONLY LIGHT CAN DO THAT.
HATE CANNOT DRIVE OUT HATE,
ONLY LOVE CAN DO THAT"

"DARKNESS CANNOT DRIVE OUT DARKNESS,
ONLY LIGHT CAN DO THAT.
HATE CANNOT DRIVE OUT HATE,
ONLY LOVE CAN DO THAT"

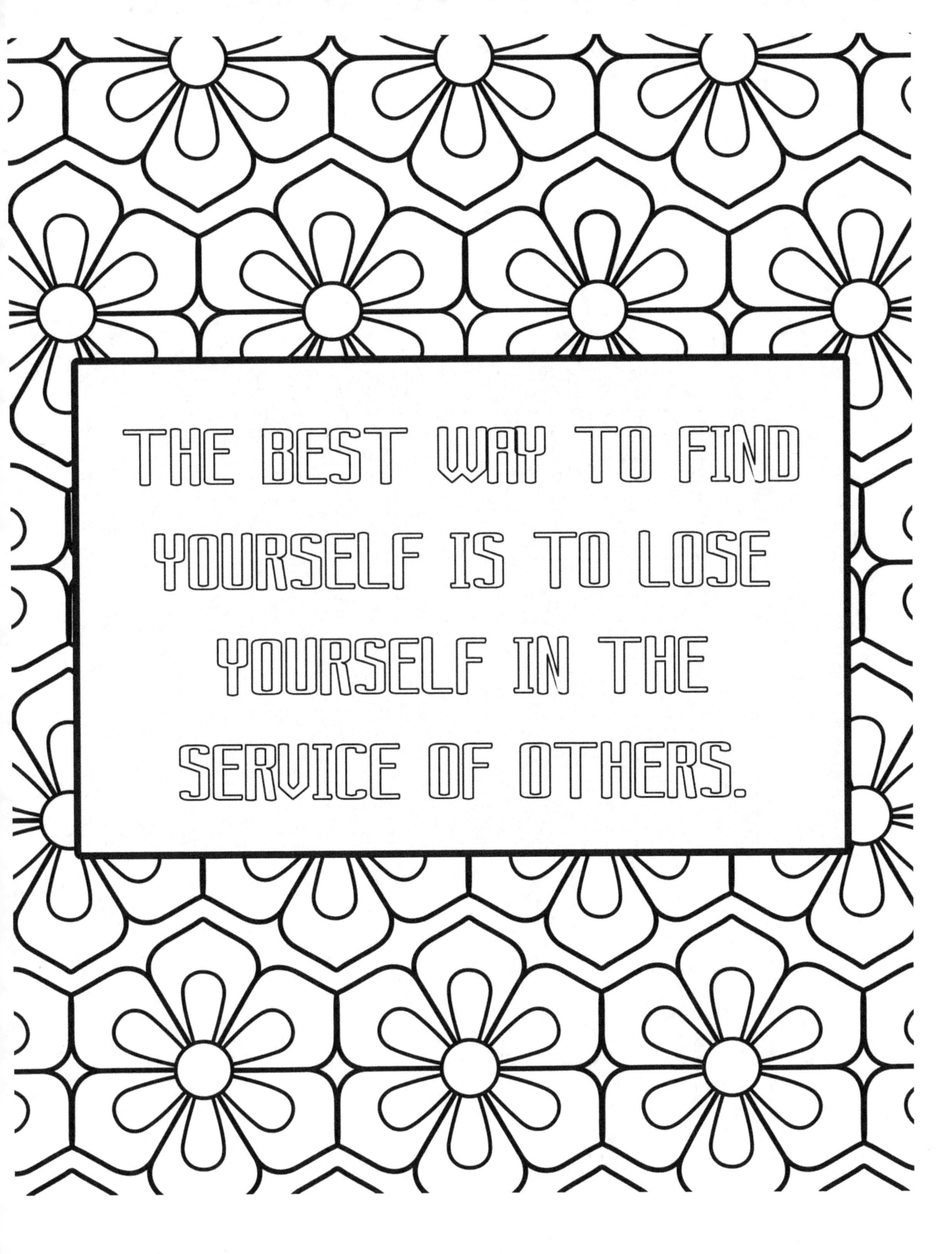

"DARKNESS CANNOT DRIVE OUT DARKNESS,
ONLY LIGHT CAN DO THAT.
HATE CANNOT DRIVE OUT HATE,
ONLY LOVE CAN DO THAT"

"DARKNESS CANNOT DRIVE OUT DARKNESS,
ONLY LIGHT CAN DO THAT.
HATE CANNOT DRIVE OUT HATE,
ONLY LOVE CAN DO THAT"

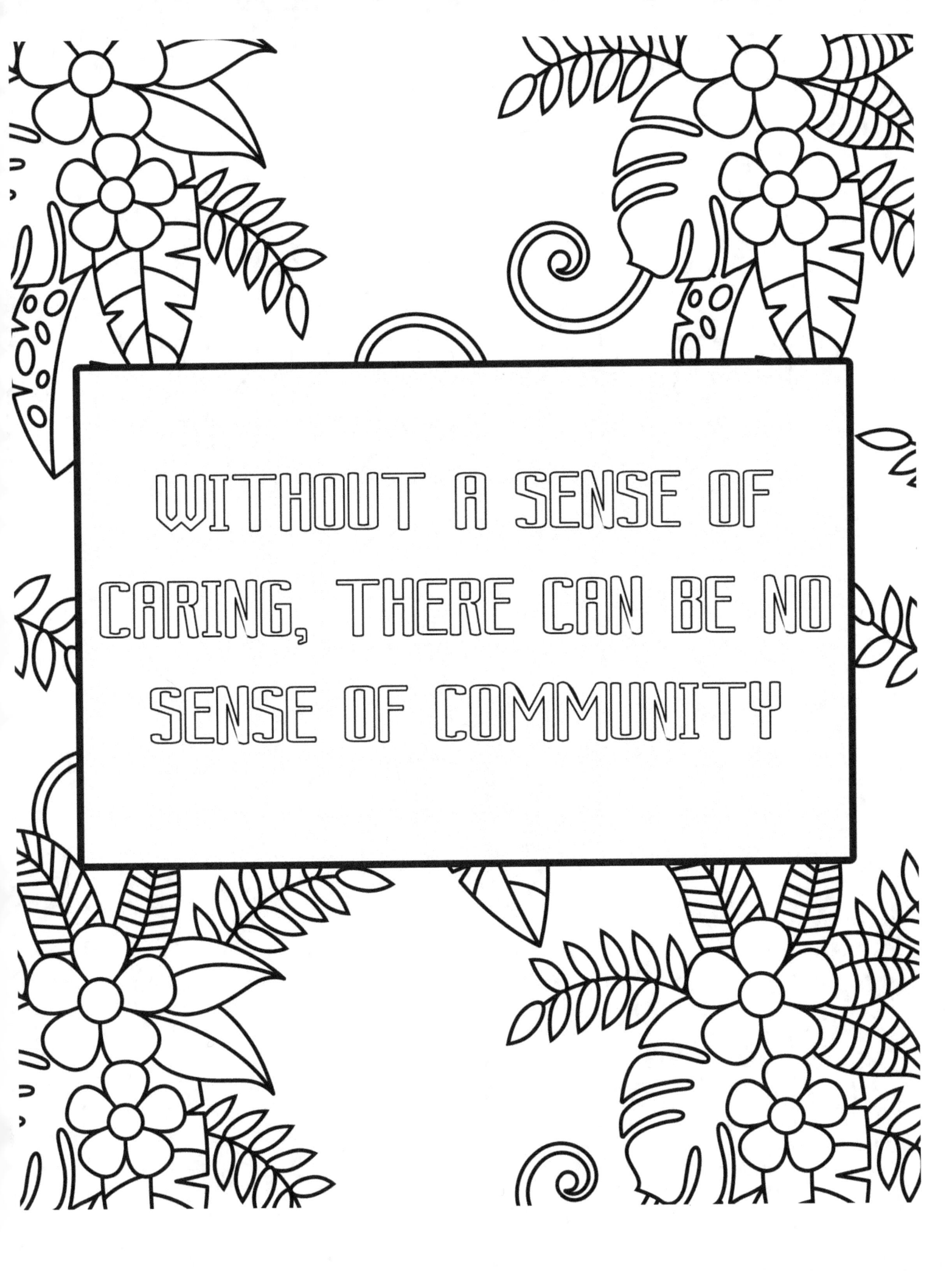

"DARKNESS CANNOT DRIVE OUT DARKNESS,
ONLY LIGHT CAN DO THAT.
HATE CANNOT DRIVE OUT HATE,
ONLY LOVE CAN DO THAT"

"DARKNESS CANNOT DRIVE OUT DARKNESS,
ONLY LIGHT CAN DO THAT.
HATE CANNOT DRIVE OUT HATE,
ONLY LOVE CAN DO THAT"

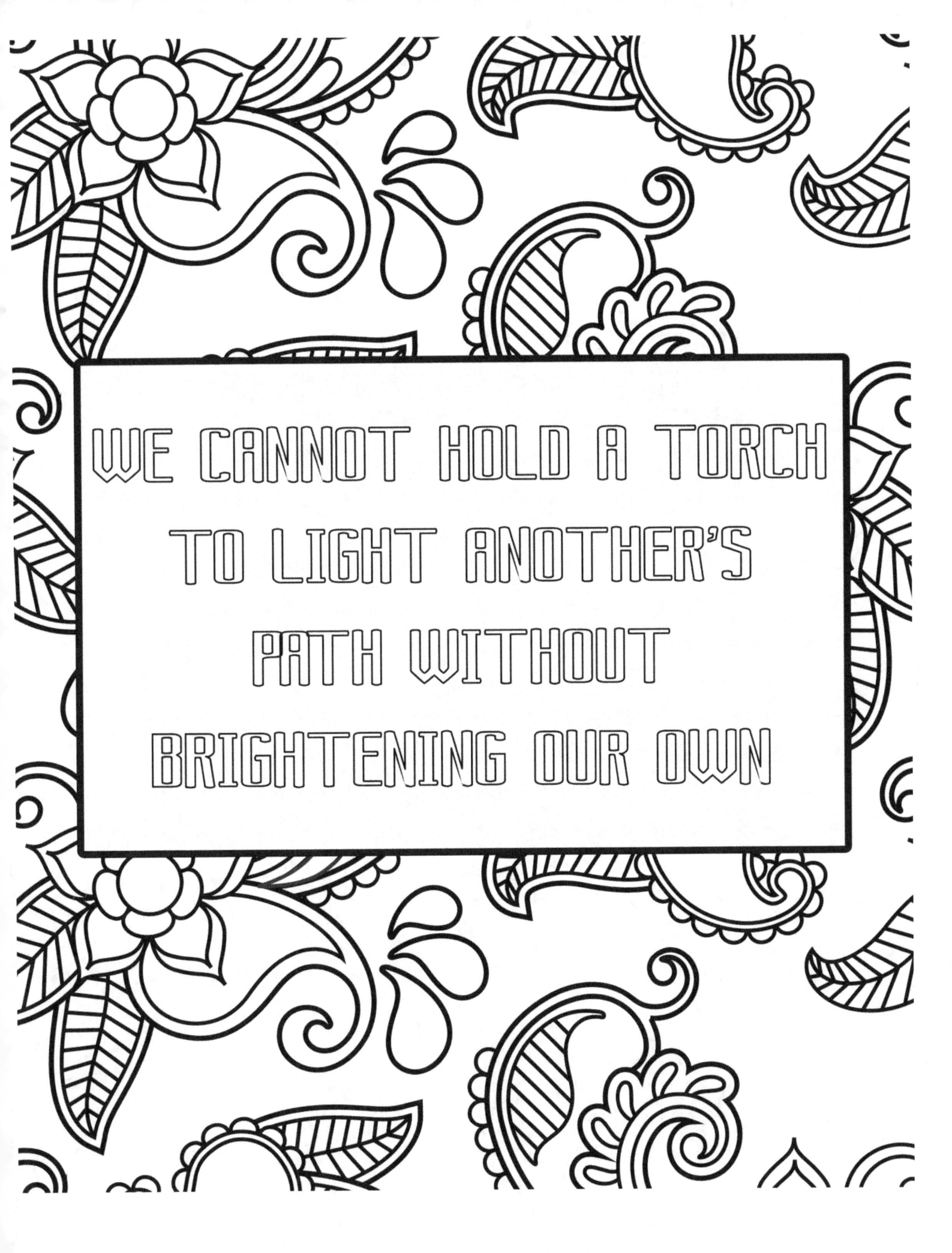

"DARKNESS CANNOT DRIVE OUT DARKNESS,
ONLY LIGHT CAN DO THAT.
HATE CANNOT DRIVE OUT HATE,
ONLY LOVE CAN DO THAT"

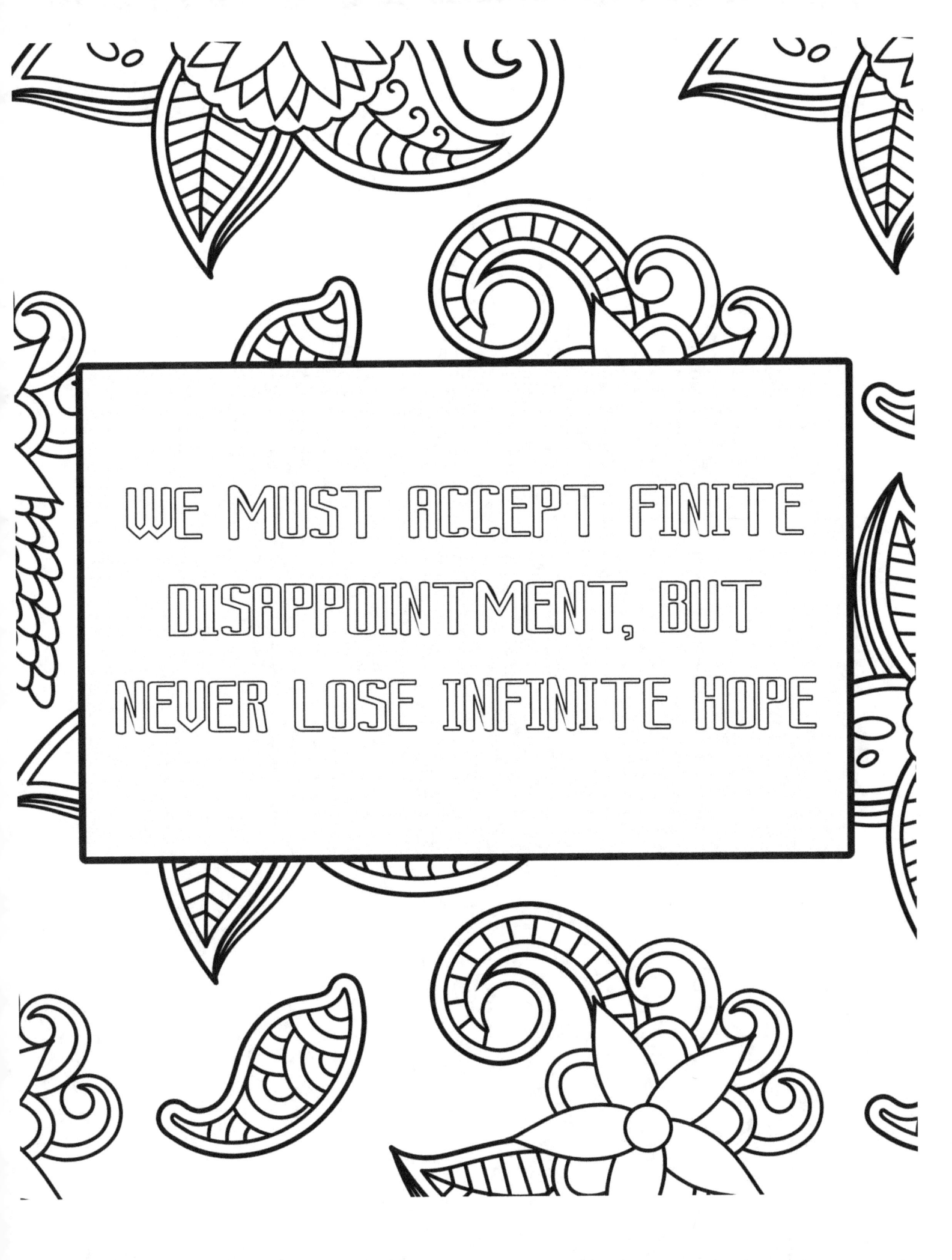

"DARKNESS CANNOT DRIVE OUT DARKNESS,
ONLY LIGHT CAN DO THAT.
HATE CANNOT DRIVE OUT HATE,
ONLY LOVE CAN DO THAT"

"DARKNESS CANNOT DRIVE OUT DARKNESS,
ONLY LIGHT CAN DO THAT.
HATE CANNOT DRIVE OUT HATE,
ONLY LOVE CAN DO THAT"

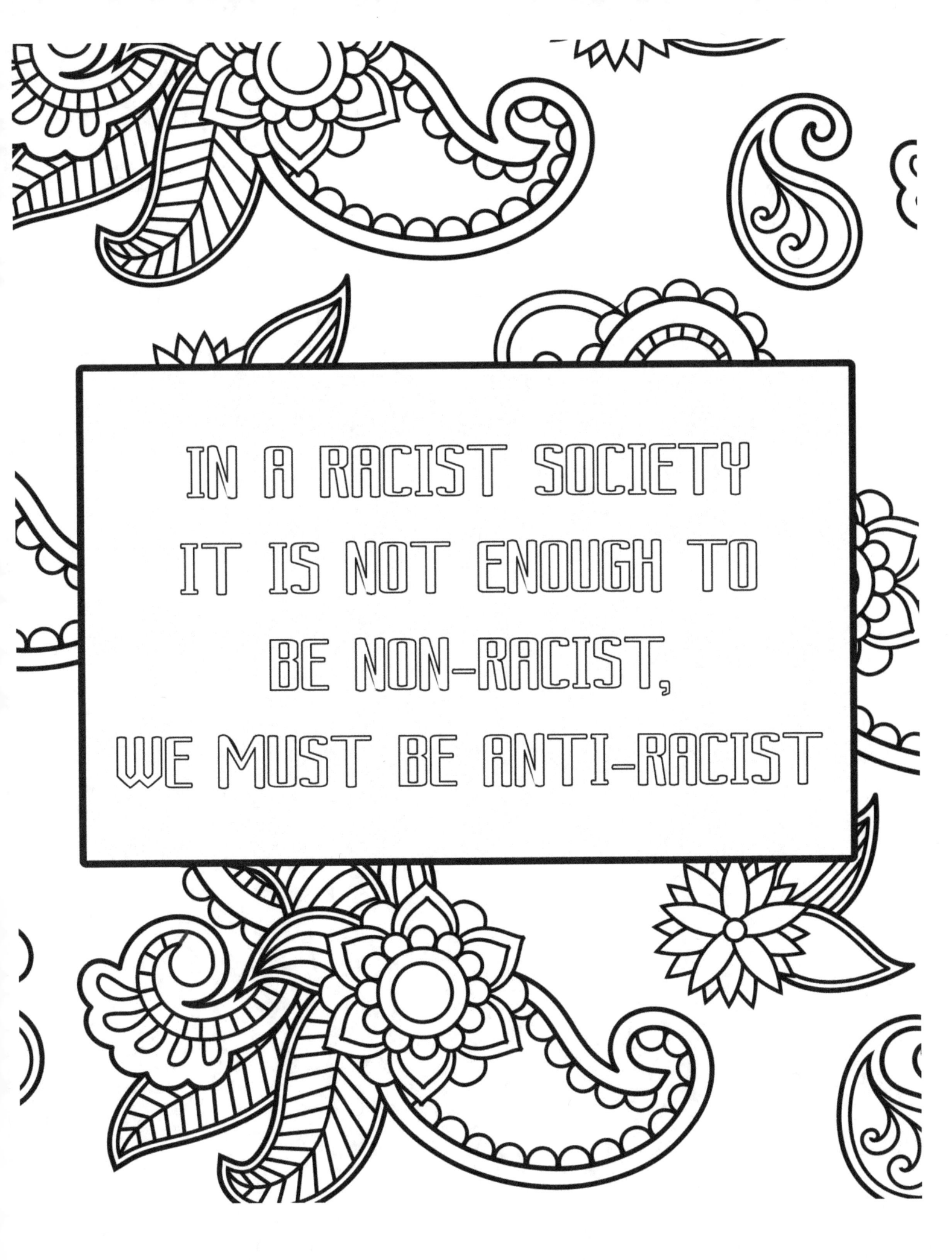

"DARKNESS CANNOT DRIVE OUT DARKNESS,
ONLY LIGHT CAN DO THAT.
HATE CANNOT DRIVE OUT HATE,
ONLY LOVE CAN DO THAT"

www.ingramcontent.com/pod-product-compliance
Lightning Source LLC
Chambersburg PA
CBHW081102240526
45465CB00026B/3254